Marital Satisfaction Guaranteed

–

13 Principles of a Lasting Marriage

John M. Hewett

Copyright 2016 By John M. Hewett
ISBN 978-1-940609-61-4 Paperback
Revised May 2018
All rights reserved
No part of this book may be reproduced or transmitted in any form or by any means, electronic or mechanical, including photocopying, recording, or by any information storage and retrieval system, without permission in writing from the copyright owner.

Thanks to Betty Stover for editing this book

This book was printed in the United States of America.
To order additional copies of this book, contact:
JohnMHewett@gmail.com

Published by FWB Publications
Columbus, Ohio

John and Kim

Dedicated to my wife Kim.

Preface

The phone rings. It's a gentleman in my congregation. He needs to talk, today. When he enters my office, he sits down on the sofa, and tears begin streaming down his face. His wife has filed for divorce, and he doesn't know what to do. He never thought it would come to this. How did it get so bad? Is there anything he can do to get his family back?

For those in pastoral ministry this scene is far too familiar. It is no news to anyone that homes are collapsing all around us. Husbands and wives are desperate for trustworthy wisdom to bring stability and joy into their marriages. Thankfully, in this little book, John Hewett has provided a wealth of biblical instruction and practical principles that promise to breathe life into marriages of all kinds. Whether you are not yet wedded but hope to have an amazing marriage someday, fighting just to keep your relationship from unraveling, or have a good marriage that you want to make great, Marital Satisfaction Guaranteed: 13 Principles of a Lasting Marriage has helpful direction for you.

John Hewett is a husband and father who practices what he preaches. I've been John's pastor for well over a decade, and his family has been an inspiration to us all. I've witnessed the Hewett family dance on the mountain tops and walk through the valley of the shadow of death, and through it all they have not wavered in their love and commitment to each other. In Marital Satisfaction Guaranteed: 13 Principles of a Lasting Marriage, John draws on years of experience as a faithful husband, caring pastor, and sage family counselor. Carefully and prayerfully journey through this book, and you can discover the joy of God's perfect plan for marriage.

Pastor Jeff Blair
Locust Grove Free Will Baptist Church
Locust Grove, Oklahoma

Table of Contents

Introduction	9
Principle 1 – Choose the Right Partner	15
Principle 2 – Put Christ First	27
Principle 3 – Cut the Cord	35
Principle 4 – Check Your Baggage	45
Principle 5 – Choose Your Responsibilities	57
Principle 6 – Choose to Forgive	65
Principle 7 - Practice Effective Communication	75
Principle 8 – Care for One Another's Needs	87
Principle 9 – Handle Conflict Like Adults	93
Principle 10 – Continue to Court	99
Principle 11 – Honor Your Commitment	107
Principle 12 - Persevere Through Crisis	113
Principle 13 – Cover Everything with Love	121

Marital Satisfaction Guaranteed

13 Principles of a Lasting Marriage

Introduction

"Satisfaction Guaranteed"

I confess, I am often skeptical when I see or hear those words. I think of the phrase, "There are no guarantees in life." Though that is not always the case, I fear it often is.

The reason for this skepticism is the frivolous use of the phrase. Salesmen and advertisers often offer guarantees simply to make a sale. If you are not satisfied, they figure the chances are you will just let it go, or they will just find a way to not honor their promise.

This is not the case here, however. I guarantee you, if you and your companion will apply the thirteen principles outlined in this book, you will experience a satisfying marriage. If you are not completely satisfied, return your book and an explanation of why you are not satisfied, and I will refund your money.

I promise you, this has nothing to do with making a sale. I am that sold on these concepts. They have worked on my marriage and many others over the centuries. I personally guarantee you, if you will apply the concepts of this book to your marriage, you will have a lasting and satisfying marriage.

A Smoking Hot Encounter

Kim was smoking hot when I saw her for the first time. Well, her car was. (Of course, she wasn't bad either).

I had planned on attending college at Hillsdale (Randall) in Moore, OK. Kim had planned on attending Free Will Baptist Bible College (Welch College) in Nashville, TN.

Instead, here we were in the parking lot of Arkansas Tech University in Russellville, AR. I was a senior helping freshman girls move into their dorm rooms (totally pure motives). She was a freshman just now moving onto campus.

As she drove onto the parking lot, her old Plymouth Volare was spitting and sputtering with smoke streaming from under the hood. She looked so pitiful as she got out of her car. This was not how she wanted to start off on her first day of college.

I couldn't help but feel sorry for her. Being the chivalrous gentleman I was, I ran over, popped her hood, looked at her engine for a minute, and said, "Let me go find somebody who knows something about cars."

That was it. That was the beginning of what would become a whirlwind romance. We would meet again in two weeks, be engaged within three months, and married within ten months.

That was over 30 years ago. We have been through a lot since then, but we have survived. We have done more than survive. We have actually enjoyed our time together....mostly anyway.

Don't misunderstand me. It hasn't all been easy. There have been some difficult times. We have faced many of the same struggles as so many others. We have experienced financial woes, sickness, and loss. We have disagreed, argued, and even yelled at each other.

Yes, we have yelled. We have yelled and screamed and even said some things we should not have said. To be honest, I do not speak to you as an expert that has done it all right. I speak to you as a fellow human being that has learned through my mistakes.

Folks, marriage isn't easy. Anyone who says it is easy is either a liar or does not know what they are talking about.

Becoming One

While I am on this subject, let me warn you about something. The next time someone offers you marital advice and they start off with, "My (spouse) and I have been married for (???) years and have never argued once," do not listen to another word they have to say. They are either lying or have never experienced the fullness of marriage.

Marriage is about two distinct individuals becoming one. Disagreement and discussion are absolutely necessary in marriage if two unique beings coming from different backgrounds with different personalities and paradigms are to unite together as one.

To try to pass marriage off as an easy task is a disservice. Marriage is difficult work. If you want to make it work, you must be willing to roll your sleeves up, dig your heels in, and weather the storms.

To build a wood frame house you don't simply cut down some trees, throw them together and expect to have a finished product. No, you cut them, prune them, and slice them up into lumber of different sizes. When everything is finished and pieced together just right, then you have a finished product worthy of moving into. The end result is worth every ounce of effort put forth.

Yes, Kim and I have had our share of difficulties. We have each made the needed concessions and now fit together very well though. I'm sure there is more growth yet to come, more whittling and pruning needed, but our love has grown. We once dreamed of being two people, living in harmony. Today, instead we are uniting continually as one.

The Key to Longevity in Marriage

I recently surveyed numerous couples who have been happily married for over a decade, asking them what they felt the key to their longevity and satisfaction in marriage was. The responses were varied, likely reflecting their own situation, paradigm, and experience. There were several concepts that appeared numerous times, though.

Following are several of those concepts as well as a few of my own. These are all principles Kim and I have applied to our marriage. When we have faltered in our application of them, our marriage has faltered. When these principles have been applied, our marriage has blossomed.

I challenge you to apply these concepts to your marriage. I promise you if you do, you will get positive results. Remember, Marital Satisfaction Guaranteed…

Principle 1

CHOOSE THE RIGHT PARTNER

The first step in securing a lasting marriage is choosing the right partner. I know that is easy for me to say. I hit the jackpot! Well, better put, I discovered my treasure. One might say finding Kim was pure luck, or that it was a chance encounter that I ran into her in that parking lot that day. That is not at all the case, though.

There is no doubt I was fortunate; I was blessed. I had been searching for my treasure or soul mate for years. I had even had a couple semi-serious relationships that had not worked out. I knew what I was looking for and was not settling for less. I entered my senior year with full intentions of discovering my soulmate. God directed my search. I found my treasure in the middle of the parking lot that day.

Kim is everything I'm not. She is more organized, quiet, and very deliberate. I am generally rattled, loud, and shoot from the seat of my britches. Through time, though, we each have given, taken, and blended as a whole.

As a couple, we are organized, but we are also flexible enough to adapt as needed. We are outspoken when necessary—but not obnoxious. We plan things better than I ever dreamed, but we are ready to act as circumstances dictate. You see, we are much better as a couple than we could ever be as two distinct individuals.

You can find that right person too, the one who completes you where you fall short and the one you complete as well. The key is taking your time and doing it right—which may at times mean *waiting*. The principles outlined in this book will help you do that.

Make Sure the CHEMISTRY is RIGHT

I know this one can just about go unsaid. In today's society, it almost receives too much emphasis. Chemistry is important, though. If your partner doesn't make your toes tingle now, he/she certainly will not in 20-30 years.

There was something special about the time I first met my future wife. I remember the pounding of my heart the first time we talked...the tingling the first time we touched....the flood of emotions the first time we kissed. I still enjoy holding her hand or embracing her in my arms today.

I recall a girl I dated in high school. She was nice and we shared common interests. We seemingly even shared common values. Everybody thought we were meant to be together, that our relationship must have been of God. We did not have the chemistry, though. I tried to feel it, but it just was t meant to be. Fortunately, I eventually broke it off.

Marriage is meant to be mutually enjoyed. I truly believe if God wants us together He will cause us to enjoy being together. He will, indeed, place us with a partner that we will enjoy.

COURT before you COMMIT

Take time to get to know each other. I'm not talking physically either. The longer you put that off the better it will be when it finally happens....I promise.

Start off by just hanging out together with friends. Then maybe get to know each other's families. After that, then start dating and spending time alone.

Developing a relationship is like cooking a pot roast. If you turn the burner up, you might get to experience it sooner, but you probably won't enjoy it nearly as much as you would if you let it simmer a bit.

Look for CHARACTER

Chemistry is important, but it isn't everything. The fact that he or she makes you feel good, doesn't make him or her good for you.

Character can be defined as who somebody is or becomes behind closed doors or when they think nobody is watching. It is no doubt the most difficult quality to delineate, yet the most predictive factor of how a future spouse will treat you after you are married, and 5 or 10 years down the road.

Before getting into a serious relationship with someone there are several questions you might ask yourself:

- Is this the kind of person you want to spend the rest of your life with?

- Will he/she be a good parent to your children?

- Will he/she treat you with the respect you deserve?

- Can this person be trusted?

- Will he/she stick with you through thick and thin?

Granted, these questions are difficult to answer with a simple general observation. Here are some precautions you can take that will at least give you a good indication whether that person you choose is a person of character:

- **Take a reasonable amount of time to get to know them properly** - There is not a set time frame for courting and engagement. You need to take time to at least observe them in various life crisis and circumstances. Do not take so much time that you grow weary in waiting, though.

- **Take care where you meet them** – You have a better chance of meeting someone of positive character at church or a community event than at a bar or online.

- **Take note who they run with** – If they run with individuals of questionable character, they are probably of questionable character themselves.

- **Listen to what others say** – If those who care about you have doubts, they probably have good reason. Trust your family and friends more than you do your hormones.

Remember, what may seem cute now could haunt you in the future. You can't count on your mate to change. Make sure you are marrying him/her for who he/she is, not for who you hope he/she may become.

Complete Each Other

We often hear that opposites attract. There is, no doubt, an element of truth to this assumption. The Bible teaches that Adam was incomplete without Eve. Her strengths complemented his weaknesses and vice versa.

I do not believe that it is necessary to be opposites, nor is it even healthy. I do believe though that it is necessary to be different. That is how we complete each other. Where he is weak she is strong and where she is weak he is strong. United they are complete.

Kim and I have many differences. As I've already pointed out, she is more introverted and I am more extroverted (though those roles appear to be reversing over the years). She likes chick flicks. I like action movies. She is well organized whereas I am totally disorganized. The list goes on.

You can see where these differences could be helpful in a marriage. Where she is somewhat shy; I never meet a stranger. Often, I am the one who must speak on our behalf. As far as organization, my mama often said I would lose my head if it wasn't screwed on. Kim helps me keep my head screwed on straight.

Share Common Interests

As different as we are, we have common interests that are kind of the glue that binds us together. We both enjoy sports...sort of. She enjoys pulling for a team whereas I enjoy watching the game. We both like music. We both like to travel and we both love kids. We also both enjoy church and ministry.

Do the same things make you smile? Make sure you have at least some shared hobbies and/or interests. Are you willing to develop and nurture new interests based on those of your partner? Are you willing to give up any hobbies or interests that might be a distraction to your relationship? Is your partner willing to do the same?

Kim and I have managed to compromise on our differences and develop new like interests over the years. A good example of this is our differing tastes in tv shows and movies. She likes romance and I like action, so we compromise and watch police dramas that include both romance and action, such as *Castle*. We both enjoy it, and it is time shared.

SHARE COMMON VALUES

I had been dating another girl casually for several months when I met Kim. This girl was attractive and fun to be with. Consequently, I invited her to a social event one evening after I had become acquainted with Kim. I came to a crossroad when

Kim showed up at my house obviously planning to attend it with me. I had to make a decision.

Kim was a Christian and Free Will Baptist like me. The other girl came from a different denomination and I wasn't even sure she was a Christian. It should have been an easy decision, but I actually struggled with it a bit. Obviously, I made the right decision though and have not regretted it for a moment.

You can differ on interests and even possibly survive without the perfect chemistry. Common values are essential, though. Marriage is a journey. You can disagree on the route and even the mode of travel, but it is absolutely necessary you are at least heading the same direction.

- **Do you share the same dreams?**

When we married, Kim and I agreed that we would go anywhere God led us and do anything He led us to do. We originally envisioned that being in the Army chaplaincy or even on the mission field. We ended up in the pastoral ministry for the first 15 years of our marriage. Following that, we have continued ministry from various platforms over the years.

Granted, your dreams should bear some flexibility, but they should both at least be aimed the same general direction. What do you envision accomplishing in life? Does your spouse or prospective spouse share that vision? You really need to iron this one out if you wish for your marriage to last.

- **Do you possess the same drive?**

I am motivated by charity, as is Kim. Fortunately, she is not high maintenance. If she were she would be long overdue for scheduled maintenance.

Are you motivated by financial gain, ambition, popularity, or compassion, etc.? It is important you possess the same or compatible drive as your partner or your relationship may be torn apart by conflicting motivations.

- **Do you envision the same future for your family?**

What do you envision your family looking like in 5, 10, 15 years? How many children do you plan to have? When do you plan to start your family?

We didn't plan on having six children, but we both wanted a large family. If one of you dreams of having a household full of children running around within the first five years of marriage and the other dreams of spending those first five years getting to know each other, somebody is no doubt going to be disappointed,

- **Do you share a common faith?**

I'm not saying where and if you go to church affects your likelihood of marital satisfaction and/or longevity. Some say it doesn't. What I am saying here is, if your faith is important to you, it needs to be shared by your partner. If faith and/or religion makes you uncomfortable, you are best to avoid a serious relationship with someone of deep faith.

Kim and I are both believers and from the same denomination. I am not saying our denomination is better than yours. I am saying that that is one disagreement we have never had. We have always known we were going to church and pretty much where we were going.

How important is faith to you? What are the non-negotiables? Does your partner share these same convictions? If not, how do you plan to make it work?

****

Starting off right does not guarantee a successful marriage. Starting off wrong though does just about guarantee struggles down the road. Start off as I have outlined here, and you will definitely have a head start on a long and fulfilling relationship.

2 Cor 6:14-16

Activity that Promotes Longevity and Satisfaction...

Plan an activity that neither of you has done before based on your like interests and differences that complement each other. Discuss your differences based on this chapter and how you have and plan to overcome those differences. Following, is questionnaire that might be especially helpful for single person searching for their life partner.

CHOOSE the RIGHT MATE Questionnaire:

Do I enjoy being with this person? / Does he/she make my toes tingle?

Have we taken time to get to know each other?

Is this the kind of person I want to spend the rest of my life with?

Will he/she be a good parent to my children?

Will he/she treat me with the respect i deserve?

Can this person be trusted?

Will he/she stick with me through thick and thin?

Where did I meet him/her?

What kind of people does he/she run with?

What do my friends and family think of him/her?

Do our strengths and weaknesses compliment each other?

Do we share common interests?

Do we share the same dreams?

Do we possess the same drive?

Do we envision the same future?

Do we share a common faith?

Principle 2

PUT CHRIST FIRST

"Unless the Lord builds the house, they labor in vain who build it." Psalm 127:1

You can apply the ten or eleven not-so-spiritual principles of this book to your marriage and find satisfaction in this life even without Christ. Satisfaction in this life alone is vain and shortsighted, though. Ultimate satisfaction or fulfillment in marriage comes only as we put Christ first.

From the time we were married, Kim and I told God we would go anywhere He called us to go and do anything He told us to do. We have not always been the perfect Christian couple, praying and studying together as we should, but we have always made that our goal and we have been blessed accordingly.

Following are several steps that will help you as a couple grow in Christ. These steps are not all inclusive nor are they foolproof. Thank God He is a gracious God though, and willing to take us as we are and make us into what we can ultimately become.

1. Possess a Personal Relationship with Christ

Acts 16:31 "Believe on the Lord Jesus Christ, and you will be saved, you and your household."

Each spouse is responsible for his/her own personal relationship with Christ. You may influence your spouse by your faith. You cannot save your spouse by your faith though, nor does your spouse's faith save you. It is a personal issue.

Paul said in 1 Corinthians 15:19, "If in this life only we have hope in Christ, we are of all men the most pitiable (miserable)." If you find great happiness in your marriage and yet do not find Christ, your happiness will be shallow and short lived. The key to true happiness is found in Christ, not in the perfect marriage. Happiness discovered in Christ will in turn result in a satisfying marriage.

2. Partner in your walk with Christ.

Ephesians 5:33 "Let every one of you in particular so love his wife even as himself; and the wife [see] that she reverence [her] husband."

1 Thessalonians 5:11 "Comfort each other and edify one another"

Though we are not responsible for each other's faith or walk with Christ, we are responsible for encouraging and edifying one another in their walk. Whether we have daily devotions or just regular discussions, we need to encourage each other in the faith.

I once put forth great effort, thought, and prayer to see a particular ministry come to fruition. When it finally did succeed, it was somebody else that received the credit for it. I was consequently hurt.

I moped around for days and weeks, disappointed that nobody knew the effort I put forth. After a while my wife got her fill of my self-absorption. One day, as I once again voiced my frustration, Kim commented quietly and with respect, "It's not about you."

I was immediately convicted. I broke down in tears and prayed for forgiveness. She had spoken only four words, but those four words were just the words I needed.

As I have ministered in various capacities over the past few decades, there have been many trials and tribulations. Satan has snapped at my heels constantly. Encouragement and sometimes correction has come from various sources, but none has been as piercing and insightful as the words offered me by my wife. Many a battle won would have been lost were it not for the inspiration of Kim. When battles have been lost, she has been there to encourage me to face the next battle.

3. Pray Together

Matthew 18:19 "Again I say to you that if two of you agree on earth concerning anything that they ask, it will be done for them by My Father in heaven."

Approximately 50% of marriages end in divorce. Sadly, those percentages aren't much better for couples that attend church. Those numbers improve significantly for those who pray together though. Some possible reasons for this improvement are as follows:

- There is **HARMONY** in Prayer. In order to pray together you must come together and agree on the topics and expectations of your prayer. This fosters harmony in your marriage.

- There is **HONESTY** in Prayer. Sharing your needs with each other for prayer opens up the avenues of communication and fosters honesty in your relationship.

- There is **HOPE** in Prayer. The expectations of prayer bring hope for better days in a relationship.

- There is **HELP** in Prayer. When we communicate our needs, we solicit God's help in our relationship. Sometimes we face more opposition in our relationship than we can handle alone. God is willing, capable, and ready to help us overcome the obstacles, if we ask.

There are several elements that need to be present in our prayer life to make it most effective:

A. Pray Regularly

Marriage is sanctioned by God; therefore, it is despised by Satan. There is nothing the devil would like more than to destroy your marriage. That is the reason regular prayer is so important.

Decide on a good time for you to pray together on a regular basis. That might be first thing in the morning or in the evening before bedtime. The most important thing is you come together in prayer regularly.

B. Pray Honestly

We are told in James 5:16 to confess our faults one to another. We need somebody to hold us accountable; somebody who knows us better than anybody else. That somebody should often be our spouse. We need to be honest and open in our prayer time, so we can hold each other up in prayer.

C. Pray Consistently

We all have periods in which we feel alone, separated from God. Couples can find themselves drifting away from each other as well. We need to pray together even when we don't feel like it and pray until we begin to feel like it again.

4. Dwell in the Presence of Other Believers

In Hebrews 11:25 we are told not to miss out on meeting together and encouraging one another. Just as we as individuals need our spouse to complete us and encourage us in our walk with Christ, we as couples need a body of believers to embrace us and walk along beside us in our walk with Christ. We can find this encouragement through church, small groups, or Sunday school. Surround yourself with those who will encourage you in your faith.

****

If you were only able to apply one of these thirteen principles to your marriage, I would hope this would be the one. It makes the application of the other principles much more natural. Putting Christ first will help you choose the right partner, give you courage to cut the cord, and guide you in checking your baggage, etc.

(Joshua 24:15)

ACTIVITY THAT PROMOTES LONGEVITY AND SATISFACTION

Set up a regular time to pray with your spouse. if you do not have a spiritual support group to encourage you in your Christian walk, explore and discuss the possibilities.

Principle 3

CUT THE CORD

I have married off two children so far. When I say, "Married off," I mean it too. I actually helped officiate their weddings, and when I let them go, I let them go.

That is what parenting is about. We prepare our children to raise their own families and/or become contributors to society in their own way. When they reach a proper level of ability and desire to do that, we let them go.

Neither of my two oldest children ended up doing with their lives what I envisioned. I dreamed of my daughter serving on the foreign mission field and my son playing professional sports. My daughter is a stay at home mom and my son is a youth minister. Both are focused on raising their own families, fulfilling their own dreams, and living their own lives. I couldn't be prouder!

Why am I proud? Because they are following their destinies and not mine. They are providing for their own families, not mooching off of my family.

They are contributing to society, not becoming a burden. They have each found their own place in life.

That is the primary purpose of parenting. You raise them to become independent, productive adults. You raise them to create their own homes. You raise them to forge their own paths and make their own impressions in the world. *You raise them to let them go.*

Interfering and difficult in-laws are a leading cause for divorce early on in marriage. I have been working with troubled couples for almost 30 years. My observation has been that just about every couple considering divorce struggles with in-law issues.

Disruption or at least distress in the young marriage occurs either when one or both sets of In-laws are not willing to let go or when one or both partners are not willing to step out on their own and bear their own responsibility. This interrupts the natural development of the new couple and of the marriage itself.

When a young couple marries, two distinct individuals become one....at least that is the intent of marriage. Not only are they to become one in the flesh, they are to unite in spirit, dreams, and emotions.

Up to this point each individual has looked to their family of origin to have these needs met:

- Their parents have provided their basic necessities of life – food, clothing, and shelter,

- They have identified with the family name,

- Their dreams have included their family, and

- It is to their family they have turned for emotional support.

This provision shifts once they are married, though. It is no longer the parents and/or siblings that meet these needs. It is the partner or spouse.

Don't misunderstand. The family of origin should still be there for you. The family is still very much needed. Their role has simply shifted. They now move into a more supportive role rather the position of dominance they once held.

- They are there to catch you if you fall, but not to carry you.

- They offer advice from time to time, but do not dictate your every move.

- They might lend a few dollars to keep the lights on, but the bills are not in their name.

- They watch the kids on occasion and even spoil them some from time to time, but they leave the raising to Mom and Dad.

When you were in the womb, you were totally and completely dependent on your mom for everything – oxygen, nutrition, and security. Times have changed, though. You are no longer in the womb. Now you should be able to breathe on your own, eat and drink on your own, and even provide your own security.

You are no longer a child. It is time to grow up and be an adult. Hopefully, now you can read, write, and even provide for yourself and your own family. If your parents have raised you right, they have over time prepared you for this very moment.

So get up, grow up, get out on your own, and give your all to your wife and children. They need you!

Genesis 2:24

••

The family isn't the only influence from the past that can haunt our relationships either. Relationships can also be haunted by past disappointments, obsessions, and unhealthy relationships.

You Need to Let Go of Past Disappointments

When I was young I struggled with low self-esteem. I was a failure academically. I struggled at sports, and I didn't fit in socially.

When I married, I was very sensitive to anything I perceived as criticism. Many an argument escalated because I perceived my wife was criticizing me or talking down to me. In reality, she was simply expressing her opinion.

As I work with couples I often uncover past failures or insecurities in one or both spouses that explain much of the arguing they do today. In order for a relationship to progress, both partners need to grow beyond past failures and insecurities. This can be accomplished by:

- **Laughing** at them. Don't take yourself too seriously. Everybody makes mistakes. Celebrate life's little mishaps with a good laugh.

- **Learning** from them. Don't make the same mistakes again.

- **Leaving** them behind. Don't allow your past failures to rob you of today's peace and tomorrow's success. Move on.

Leave Your Distracting Activities Behind

It is ok to have fun and even get away from each other to do it on occasion, but it needs to be kept in perspective. If you have to lie and manipulate in order to participate in it or if it causes undue stress to your relationship, give it up…or at least re-prioritize it.

As I address this the sitcom, "Everybody Loves Raymond", comes to mind. I think of Ray constantly coming up with excuses to go golfing with his friends, neglecting his responsibilities as a father and a husband. Golfing itself was not the problem. His problem was a distortion in priorities.

It is difficult to put a time limit on this, but remember that your family is your priority. If the only way you can have a good time is to get away, you are probably doing something wrong anyway.

- **Enjoy** some away time responsibly. It is ok to get away for a couple hours every week or so. Just keep it real.

- **Expect** your spouse to do the same. You would be shocked how many get this one all wrong. Remember, it goes both ways.

- **Enjoy** yourselves together more than not. Honestly, after thirty years with kids in the house, when we get free time, we mostly want to spend it together as a couple. Hopefully, you'll get to that point as well.

Ditch Your Unhealthy Relationships

Close to equaling the destructive influence of interfering or controlling family members is that of friends from the past. To be honest, it is hard for friendships to survive marriages. Too much has changed.

In order to survive, the friendship needs to change as well. Here are some steps that might help prevent friendship problems:

- **Initiate** boundaries. Let your friends know your family is now the number one priority in your life. Family comes first!

- **Include** them in your family activities on rare occasion. If they really want to be a part of your life, they can join you for dinner at McDonalds or Chuck E Cheese. This is probably a good way to filter out old friends, but if they are not interested in your family, they're not your real friends anyway.

- **Invite** new friends into your life as a couple and family. I personally believe this is the best option. You will enjoy time more with friends with like interests and the activities you share are more likely to be family focused.

I know these actions may seem radical. The fact is marriage and building a family are radical steps that warrant radical measures. I promise you, watching your kids grow up and celebrating thirty years of marriage makes it all worth it!

••

What I'm saying is you need to leave it all behind. You have a new life and purpose now. Life is no longer about you. It is about your spouse, children, and you as a family. For this new life, you need a totally new focus and set of priorities.

1 Cor 15:33

Activity that Promotes Longevity and Satisfaction...

Each partner determine privately and then together what part(s) of their past interferes with their present relationship. As a couple, discuss, develop, and initiate a plan of action. What activities need to be limited, eliminated, shared? What about relationships? What can you do to forge new activities and relationships together? Approach and discuss the following contract with your extended family or other family of support.

FAMILY SUPPORT CONTRACT

Understanding the commitment

_____ and _____

have made to each other in marriage and knowing the difficulties that lie ahead, we pledge our undivided support to them. Also understanding this is their walk and their challenge, though we pledge our support to them, we make it our promise not to get in their way.

- We will try to catch them if and when they fall, but we will not carry them all along the way.

- We will offer words of wisdom and advice from time to time, but will not try to dictate their every move.

- We might lend a few dollars when we can afford to to help keep the lights on or for some other need, but the bills will not be in our name, etc.

- We might watch the kids on occasion and even spoil them some from time to time, but we will leave the raising to Mom and Dad.

We acknowledge the above are just examples of what might be needed. We will do whatever we can to help them obtain Marital Satisfaction, but we will not get in the way of their marital independence.

Signed:

Principal 4

CHECK YOUR BAGGAGE

My family likes to travel. More specifically, we like to travel by air.

One of the more difficult tasks of flying is getting to and from your location with limited baggage. The airlines will generally allow only one or two checked bags and a carry-on.

Getting there is generally not so bad. There is usually plenty of room in the beginning. Getting back can be a different story though, with additional baggage, such as souvenirs and necessities accumulated along the way.

At one point or another we must decide what is worth keeping. Only after we have eliminated our excess baggage is there enough room for whatever additional items we are sure to accumulate along the way.

This is similar to how we store our emotional baggage through life. When we are born, we are given two checked bags and a carry-on...no more, no less.

In these bags, we store all our negative emotions that are not processed or resolved otherwise. It is seemingly easier to store them than deal with them.

In the beginning, there is plenty of room to store everything. There is almost too much room. We find it so easy to stuff our emotions down in the bottom of the bag that we basically forget about them...for the time being anyway.

In time though, our bags begin to fill, and we find it more and more difficult to find space to stuff any additional emotions. Before we know it, we have crammed so much in our bags that the zipper is ripping, and our negative emotions are popping out everywhere. We get to the point we can no longer contain even the smallest piece of baggage or emotion.

This leads to what I call hyper-emotionalism. The waitress gets our order wrong and we go ballistic. We lose $5 in the parking lot and we have a nervous fit. We are passed over for a promotion at work and we just about give up on life. Our reaction is unequal to the circumstances.

When we marry, we no doubt bring baggage with us; some of us more, some of us less, but all of us carry in baggage. This baggage can sometimes be a great detriment to marital satisfaction. When our bags are full of unresolved emotions, there is no more room for even the smallest infraction. Consequently, when our spouse offends even ever so slightly, we lash out. There is no room to store that offense, so our only option appears to be to immediately act on it.

She asks why you are running late and you go off on a tirade, claiming she never trusts you. He asks what is for supper and you go off on him, screaming and yelling he takes you for granted. What should be easily resolved or totally ignored leads to a major crisis. You simply have no room to store even the smallest infraction. What might have been a minor disagreement can land you in divorce court.

5 Steps to Cleaning the Negative Emotions Out of Your Bags

Over the next few pages, I intend to help you identify your negative emotions and lighten your load. Well, I will do my part. It is up to you to unzip your bags, look through the contents, and get rid of that unnecessary baggage.

There are several steps to emptying your emotional baggage. You take these steps, you will not only increase your satisfaction in marriage, and you will increase your satisfaction in life.

1. Take a Personal Inventory

The first step to lightening your load is identifying your excess baggage. Once you identify it, you can figure out what to do with it.

The emotions we address here are anger, fear, and sadness. Of course, these three emotions do not account for all possible negative emotions. Just about every negative emotion is related to one of these three emotions though.

A. Anger

The first emotion we are going to look for among your baggage is anger. In and of itself anger is not bad. It is simply an emotional response to a perceived threat. Uncontrolled anger is like a cancer though. It starts off small, then spreads throughout your soul, eating away at your very being. Before long it has totally consumed you. If it consumes you, it will consume your marriage too. Answer these following questions and discover if anger is a problem for you:

- Do you carry resentment for past offenses? (Abuse, rejection, neglect, etc.)

- Do you need to forgive somebody for causing you pain? (Your lack of forgiveness hurts only you.)

- Are you angry with God for your circumstances? (You might as well own up to it. He knows anyway.)

- Do you possess unresolved anger of any kind that you can think of?

- Do you fly off the handle or get irritated over the smallest of offenses?

If you said yes to any of these questions, anger is apparently a problem for you and will likely prevent you from having a fully satisfying marriage; that is, unless you get rid of it. If anger is a problem for you, go to step two and take ownership of it, then follow the remaining steps to get rid of it.

B. Fear

Fear is the sense of impending danger, whether real or imagined. Like anger, it will keep you from experiencing life to its fullest. It will keep you from ever fully trusting anyone, particularly your spouse. Answer the following questions and discover if fear is a hindrance to you experiencing marital satisfaction.

- Have you ever experienced a trauma or crisis that haunts you even today with nightmares or flashbacks?

- Do you have irrational fears that you may or may not be able to trace back to your past?

- Do you experience unexplained anxiety (sensation of impending doom) or anxiety attacks?

If you answered yes to any of the above, you are evidently experiencing problems with fear or anxiety. As I said before, this can affect your marriage, as well as you personally. Follow the next few steps after 'C' and experience life and marriage without excessive fear.

C. Sadness

Everybody experiences periodic sadness in their life. It is a normal reaction to adverse circumstances or events. To try to live a life without sadness is unrealistic and unhealthy.

That said, to allow sadness to take over your life and cast a shadow over all that you see and do is even worse. No matter how bad things seem, there is always good to be found. Acknowledge the bad, but focus on the good.

Let's discover and address what makes you sad. Like you did concerning anger and fear, answer the following questions and let's see if you struggle with sadness.

- Have you experienced a loss that brings you sadness when you are reminded about it?

- Do you generally feel sad and uninterested in things that used to peak your interest?

- Have you reached a point in life that all seems hopeless?

If you answered yes to any of the above, you are struggling with sadness. As I said before, this can affect your marriage, as well as you personally. Follow the next few steps and experience life and marriage without unhealthy sadness.

2. Take Personal Responsibility

Do not allow yourself to become enslaved by your emotions or the offenders in your life. Events, people, and circumstances might elicit certain emotions. You determine what you will do with or about those emotions. As long as you blame others or your circumstances for the way you feel, you remain enslaved by your feelings.

Bad things happen to everybody. Each person determines the effect they are going to allow those circumstances to have on their life though. Do not allow your emotions to control your thoughts and reactions. Instead, control your emotions and actions with your thoughts.

3. Picture Life Without the Negative Emotion

Imagine life without the negative emotion(s). What would be different or better if you weren't struggling with this emotional baggage? How would you react to contrary circumstances? How would your relationship be improved or look? Imagine life without the negative emotion, then make your imagination a reality.

4. Pray for Peace

Pray that God give you peace in place of your negative emotions. If you do this with sincerity, you will discover a peace like you have never known before. (Philippians 4:7)

5. Proceed Without the Negative Emotion

The world is full of those who have rid themselves of negative emotions only to allow them to return bigger and stronger than before. Do not allow the negative emotions to return. Replace them with positive emotions and carry on with life victoriously.

Remember, these three emotions we have discussed are just that, emotions. They do not mandate our actions. They only influence them. We decide how we will react.

****

As was pointed out in step five, ridding oneself of negative thoughts and emotions does not guarantee they will not return. You must fill the void left by them with the positive, leaving no room for their return. (Philippians 4:8-9)

ACTIVITY THAT PROMOTES LONGEVITY AND SATISFACTION

As individuals, go through steps 1-5 on the following guide over and over until you have rid yourself of all unwanted baggage.

CLEANING OUT YOUR BAGGAGE

1. **Take a Personal Inventory...**
   A. Do You Have Unresolved ANGER?
   - Do you carry resentment for past offenses?
   - Do you need to forgive somebody for causing you pain?
   - Are you angry with God for your circumstances?
   - Do you possess unresolved anger of any kind?
   - Do you fly off the handle or get irritated over the smallest of offenses?

If you said yes to any of these questions, anger is a problem for you. Go to step two and follow the remaining steps to get rid of it.

   B. Do You Possess Unhealthy FEAR?
   - Have you ever experienced a trauma that haunts you even today?
   - Do you have irrational fears that you trace to your past?
   - Do you experience unexplained anxiety or anxiety attacks?

If you said yes to any of these questions, anxiety is a problem for you. Go to step two and follow the remaining steps to get rid of it.

C. Are You Overwhelmed By Sadness?
- Have you experienced a loss that brings you sadness when reminded of it?
- Do you feel sad and uninterested in things that used to peak your interest?
- Have you reached a point in life that all seems hopeless?

If you said yes to any of these questions, sadness is a problem for you. Go to step two and follow the remaining steps to get rid of it.

2. **Take Personal Responsibility** for your emotion. Do not blame others, your environment, or your circumstances.

3. **Picture Life Without the Negative Emotion.**

4. **Pray for Peace** to permeate your entire being. Phil. 4:7

5. **Proceed Without the Negative Emotion.**

*Repeat the preceding steps until you have rid your baggage of all negative emotions.

Principle 5

CHOOSE YOUR RESPONSIBILITY

Lilly and David

Lilly and David were married at a very young age. David was a pastor and Lilly was a stay at home mom. David was determined to be the breadwinner of the household as well as the decision-maker. Lilly was ok with that, as she didn't want the responsibility.

The problem was, it was a small church and did not pay well. David ended up taking on a secular job in addition to performing his pastoral duties. He would get up in the morning at about 5:30, eat a bowl of cereal, and go to work. He would get home around 5:30, eat supper, make a couple pastoral visits in the community, come back home, study a little for his messages, then go to bed, only to start the same routine again the next day. He was able to maintain this pace for a short while, but it eventually began to take its toll on him, his marriage, and his ministry.

Lilly struggled as well. She tried her best to manage the household but lacked motivation with her husband hardly ever home. She began to resent her husband and the church for the predicament her and her husband were in. This was not what she had envisioned marriage to be.

One day the young couple was visited by Sister Ethel, a wise elderly church member. Sister Ethel confided that she was concerned for their wellbeing. She feared if they did not make some changes, their marriage and ministry were going to continue to decay and eventually fall apart. She suggested they rethink how they shared their responsibilities in the home.

These words of wisdom were difficult to swallow, but David and Lilly knew they were true. They prayed for God's guidance and ended up making some drastic changes.

Lilly went to work part time waitressing at a local diner. David quit his job and dedicated his time to pastoring the church and caring for the household. Though their arrangement was unorthodox, it worked. They struggled a little financially in the beginning, but with David's renewed focus, the church and, consequently, David's salary grew. In the end, they were both much happier as well as more productive.

"Submitting One to Another"

I was under the impression as a young man that the woman's place was in the home cooking, cleaning, and taking care of the kids. The man was the breadwinner, working in the yard, and making all the big decisions. Fortunately, this philosophy evolved through time.

I have discovered that the proper division of household duties has more to do with strengths and abilities than gender or anything else. I have witnessed satisfied households in which the husband has done most if not all the cooking and the wife has done the budgeting. I have even known families in which Dad stayed at home and cared for the kids while Mom worked outside the home as the primary breadwinner and this worked very well for them.

A couple functions best when each partner performs the duties in which he/she is best equipped to serve. Below are three criteria that might be helpful in determining which areas of responsibility in which each of you are best equipped to serve:

1. **Practicality** - Will it work? For example, in Lilly's and David's situation had the church been opposed to women working outside the home, their nontraditional arrangement would not have been practical.

2. **Passion** – Which partner possesses the greatest passion for the task? If the husband loves cooking, maybe let him at least cook

supper or Sunday dinner. If the wife loves crunching numbers, by all means let her handle the budgeting and bill paying.

3. **Potential** – Who has the greatest potential to perform the task? In the previous two examples if the husband grew up cooking for his siblings yet the wife never stepped foot in the kitchen, the husband is obviously equipped to do the cooking. If the wife majored in business math in college, she is the obvious choice for handling the budget and bills.

Here is a partial list of household responsibilities. Apply the above three criteria to determine who is best equipped to perform each responsibility:

- Handle the Finances
- Clean the House
- Prepare the Meals
- Shuttle the Kids
- Care for the Yard
- Perform Maintenance

Understand though, just because one spouse holds a certain responsibility does not mean he/she can't use some help performing it. These responsibilities can and should be shared responsibilities. A couple is a team. If they will perform as a team, they will achieve much more.

The following steps will help you work as a team:

1. **Hold up Your End of the Bargain.** Take pride in your responsibility. If yard care is what you do, strive to have the best kept yard in the neighborhood. If you are the cook, check out new recipes, and serve only the best for your family. What you do is important, and your family is counting on you to do your best.

2. **Honor Your Partner's Contribution.** We tend to think what we do is the most important task. Remember, your partner's contribution is important too. Express your appreciation regularly. Also, respect their expertise in what they do. Try not to second guess their contribution.

3. **Help When You Can, and When Your Help is Needed.** Sometimes, our tasks can become overwhelming. Be willing to lend a helping hand when possible and needed. Remember though, you are to help, not take over.

My son recently went to work at a fast food restaurant. One of the first things the management did was assign him certain duties to perform and trained him in them. He does not do everything. He has his areas of responsibility, as does the rest of the crew. If everybody does their part, the end result is satisfied customers and consequently higher sells.

A family functions similarly. No one person can do everything. If each person does their part, though, the end result is a satisfied family.

■■

Ephesians 5:21

ACTIVITY THAT PROMOTES LONGEVITY AND SATISFACTION

On the following check sheet, use the three criteria and determine who might best perform each responsibility.

RESPONSIBILITY CHECKLIST

Go through the various responsibilities of the home and use the three criteria to see who best fits that responsibility:

Handle the Finances
Passion
Practical
Potential

Clean the House
Passion
Practical
Potential

Prepare the Meals
Passion
Practical
Potential

Shuttle the Kids
Passion
Practical
Potential

Care for the Yard
Passion
Practical
Potential

Perform Maintenance
Passion
Practical
Potential

Principle 6

FORGIVE PAST AND PRESENT HURTS

Cindy was a young lady I tried to help several years back. I officiated her wedding some fifteen years ago. About five years later, her spouse contacted me and said they were having difficulties and we needed to talk.

He informed me that, in the beginning, all was well. They were happy and their intimacy was healthy. Over time, though, she had seemingly lost interest in sexual activity and eventually even started avoiding physical contact altogether.

He said he had tried everything from courting, romancing, counseling, and even backing off. Nothing seemed to help.

I met with Cindy. After several sessions, I discovered she had been sexually abused by an uncle as an adolescent.

She had forgotten the incident until after she married. At first, she thought she was just imagining it, but over time, the memories became too vivid to not be real.

This uncle was an uncle she had cared deeply about and looked up to as a father. He had stepped in and cared for her and her mom when her father ran off. She had trusted him deeply and he had betrayed that trust.

We talked about the need for forgiveness. She insisted the pain was too much. He had hurt her too deeply for her to let it go. No matter how hard I tried to convince her to let it go, she maintained that she couldn't.

After working with her for several months, she eventually quit coming to sessions. Not long after that I received word her husband had left her. She eventually remarried and they were divorced too.

Harbored resentment normally hurts only the one harboring it. Well, and then subsequently, it hurts all those who care about that person.

The lack of forgiveness will fester up like an unattended infection. It will eventually spread until it creeps into every part of your being. Your every interaction will be affected by that infection. It will bring pain to everything you say and do.

It doesn't have to be this way. You can forgive and let it go.

I know this is easier said than done—especially for something as horrible as what happened to Cindy. It takes a conscious decision on your part as well as a genuine effort to reach out to the perpetrator extending forgiveness.

Some may call this an oversimplification, but I cite four steps to forgiveness. If you will follow these four steps, not only will you be released from the pain of your past, but you will be freed to experience love in the present.

1. ACKNOWLEDGE the Pain

You have been hurt. The pain is real and the effect on your life is real. It does no good to deny it. You have experienced the pain and damage done to you to its fullest. Now acknowledge that pain and its cause to the fullest.

2. ACCUSE the Perpetrator

In order to forgive, you must first accuse the perpetrator. Unless you are fully willing to acknowledge their guilt, there is no way to forgive them. Understand, this does not require their admission of guilt (though that would no doubt make it easier). It simply requires your honest appraisal as to where the blame lies

3. ANNOUNCE Your Forgiveness

Forgive them for their offense. If you are unable to address the perpetrator in person, write them a letter, voice your forgiveness to their picture hanging on the wall, or express your forgiveness with a friend. Remember, you are not doing this to benefit the perpetrator. You are simply releasing yourself from the pain caused by the infraction.

4. LET IT GO!

That's it. Acknowledge the pain, accuse the perpetrator, and then pronounce their forgiveness. After you have forgiven the offense, LET IT GO!

Do not store it away for future use. Do not rehash the infraction and consequences every time you became a little frustrated. Once the offense has been forgiven, file it away never to be revisited.

A Testament of Forgiveness

"Can I sit here?" I heard a familiar voice asking. I turned and sure enough, it was my old breakfast buddy, David.

David is a sweet elderly gentleman I have been sharing breakfast with at the local diner for the past several years. He is an 86-year old retired carpenter-missionary who has spent much of his life serving others around the country. His wife passed away a few years back after a long battle with Alzheimer's.

Most of our time together is spent with him sharing bits of wisdom tied in with stories from his past, many of which are about his experiences with his late wife. This day was no different.

"We talked about forgiveness in Sunday School yesterday. You know where Jesus says we should forgive 7x70 times in Matthew 18:22. My wife taught me the meaning of forgiveness several years back through her life example." He went on to share her story...

His wife was abused and neglected by her birth parents for the first few years of her life, and then she and her brother were abandoned and left to fend for themselves. Eventually, they were adopted by a family near Enid, OK.

This wasn't a good situation either. They were basically treated as servants. Their parents much favored their biological children. They never celebrated her or her brother's birthdays and she basically spent her young years picking up after and caring for her siblings. Every year it got worse and into her teen years, it became unbearable.

At about 15-16 years of age, she finally had her fill and moved in with a family some 100 miles south of Enid. It was in this new community that she met David and they dated a short time. This was a much better home situation for her, but short lived.

Her younger brother got word to her that he and their adoptive father were in an altercation and he didn't think he could bear it any longer. She immediately packed her few belongings, hitched a ride to Enid and they ran away together to Texas.

That was the last Elmer heard from her for a while. Well, they did meet up on her way back through to Texas and "kissed a little, because that was what we did in those days," he said. (This brought a snicker from me)

Once in Texas, she got a job working as a waitress in a cafe. It was there she met a young man and they hit it off pretty good. He asked her out one day and she went to the movies with him. After the movie on their walk home, he kissed her and attempted more. She resisted and he raped her.

She told her brother about it and they went to talk to the judge to press charges. The judge said he could only help her if she would help him. He then made sexual advances toward her and she left with her brother. She said her brother tried to find the fellow who raped her to no avail.

A few weeks later she discovered she was pregnant. She had no one to turn to but her adoptive family. She stayed with them for a short while, and then they sent her off to a home where she was to have her baby and give it up for adoption. She was OK with that, as she knew she couldn't care for the child as she should. She eventually discovered though that her parents were actually selling her baby through this facility she was staying in. She could be no part of that so she again ran away to Texas.

In Texas, she somehow discovered a doctor who said he would deliver her baby and had a home for it. She agreed. Once again it had been a while since she and David had been together. She was scared though and gave him a call. He made his way down to meet her and sat in the car with her as she waited to go into the doctor's office.

A pleasant memory of David's is her letting him put his hand on her stomach and feel the baby move. They figured the doctor probably adopted the child but weren't sure. They continued to pray for God's blessing on the child over the years.

Of course, they did eventually marry and had four children of their own. They had a very long and happy life together. They served in the ministry together, him building and repairing churches and such and her teaching and raising their children.

David concluded his story...

"One day as she lay in the nursing home fighting for her last bits of sanity before totally succumbing to that horrid Alzheimer's, she muttered to me,

'I have forgiven them, you know.'

"I was pretty sure what she was talking about," he said, "but I asked anyway, 'Forgiven who, Sweetheart?'"

She responded simply, "All of them."

"Those were not her last words," he said. "She lived many more months following that. Her mind had been fading long before though and these were the last words of reason I recall her sharing."

What words of reason they were too! She had lived a life of peace and blessing, not because she had not experienced pain and disappointment, but because she had forgiven those who brought it upon her.

I wiped the tears from my eyes and we both sat in silence as we each finished our breakfast. I now had a new understanding of forgiveness.

FORGIVE Your PARTNER

Not only is it important that both spouses let go of transgressions from their childhood and past relationships. It is imperative that they forgive each other.

Many a marriage has been ruined by a lack of forgiveness. The victim will remain with the transgressor in spite of his/her infraction, yet will hang onto the resentment and consequent pain from past infractions relentlessly.

This is especially prevalent in cases of infidelity. Infidelity breaks the very basis of the intent of marriage. Some equate it to the unforgivable sin. It is forgivable though, and many a marriage has survived it and even come out stronger as a result. You can't survive it though, if you won't let it go.

As much as I hate divorce, I'm not convinced divorce is any greater an evil than living perpetually in resentment and spite. The infection of un-forgiveness will permeate your soul and leak into your marriage and relationships and ruin any hope for intimacy and relational happiness.

Forgiveness will release you from the infractions of the past. It will give you the freedom to enjoy the the blessings of the present and the future.

The lack of forgiveness is a festering sore that when left unattended will slowly infect an entire relationship and all those intertwined into that relationship.

Col 3:13

Activity that Promotes Longevity and Satisfaction...

Each partner, search your heart for unsettled resentment and a lack of forgiveness. Work through the steps of forgiveness and experience the freedom of forgiveness. Once you have forgiven, let it go!

Principle 7

PRACTICE EFFECTIVE COMMUNICATION

Kim and I experienced the importance of communication early on in our marriage. Valentine's Day was approaching, and we were broke. I really liked to buy her nice gifts and she knew this. Because of our financial situation, she suggested something to the effect of, "No lavish gifts this year, OK?"

That was a very simple and logical request. What she meant was that she didn't want me spending too much on gifts. What I heard though was "no gifts." Well, I went all out that year and got her absolutely nothing.

I knew I was in trouble Valentine's Day morning when I walked into the dining room and found a card lying at my place at the table. The first words out of my mouth were, "You said no gifts!"

Well, she quickly retorted that that was not what she had said. Of course, that started a vicious cycle. I became more and more defensive as did she, each of us returning potshot for potshot, to the point we ended up having a pretty heated argument.

All this could have been avoided with proper communication (or listening on my part).

Lack of communication or ineffective communication is a leading cause for marital dissatisfaction and ultimately divorce. On the flip side, effective communication is a leading component in accomplishing marital satisfaction and growth. If we cannot communicate our needs, our partner will never know what our needs are. If we cannot express our love, our love cannot be experienced.

Effective Communication Starts with Attentive Listening

Communication is as much about what you hear as what you say. You can communicate your needs only as much as you understand the listener's needs.

I have ADHD. ADHD people are notorious for looking you straight in the eyes, nodding and shaking our heads at all the right times, and even inserting an occasional well-placed "mm-hmm" or "no way" yet not listening to a word you say. Obviously, this can be a source of contention in marriage.

Kim has sent me to the store more than once to get something very specific. I have been in the car on the way to who knows where when I have suddenly realized I had absolutely no idea where I was going and what I was supposed to do when I got there. You can only imagine the frustration for her when I have called to ask her to repeat her request.

It is through listening that we gain insight into our partner's perspective. By listening attentively to what our partner has to say, we earn the right for ourselves to be heard. The lack of listening jeopardizes that right.

ATTENTIVE LISTENING is accomplished as follows:

- **RESPECT** your partner by letting them say their piece. Be patient; your turn will come.

- **REPEAT** back to them what you have heard. This ensures that what they meant to say is what you have heard them say. It also assures your partner you are truly listening.

- **RESPOND**, do not **REACT**, to what your partner has to say. Think it through before you speak. Do not just blurt out the first thing that comes to mind. Thoughtfully respond; do not haphazardly react.

LEARN to Read your Partner's Communication Cues

Communication is at least as much nonverbal as it is verbal. In other words, we communicate as much by our facial and body expressions and our tonal inflection as we do by what we say.

To illustrate this, you might call your dog to you, bend over, and say in a loving, caring voice, "I despise you, you mangy mutt. Here in a short bit, I am taking your lazy butt to the pound and letting them deal with you."

Because of your tone and presentation, the dog will likely wag his tail and even lick your face. The dog responds more to your nonverbal cues than your verbal cues. Of course, humans are not identical in their response, but they still rely heavily on nonverbal cues.

Basically, what I am saying is, if all your communication skills are based solely on verbal cues, you are destined to experience misunderstandings. You must be able to understand and communicate nonverbally in order to experience healthy growth in your relationship.

Below are what I believe to be the primary communication cues necessary for effective communication. Of course, this is not all inclusive, but if you master these three elements of communication, your communication will excel.

- **VERBAL** Communication is the basis for communication. Our words need to be mastered and carefully chosen in order to communicate effectively. Think before you speak and only speak what you have carefully thought through.

- **TONAL** Inflection either accentuates or diminishes our verbal communication. Much is said by the tone of voice we use. There is rarely any good that comes out of yelling. Simply say what you mean and mean what you say and there is no reason to be mean in how you say it.

- **FACIAL** Expression - Learn how to read your partner's face. It is in the face we express our true feelings. They may say everything is fine, but it is in their expression that the truth is revealed.

LIVE by the GOLDEN RULE of Communication –

Much like the Golden Rule of the Beatitudes, "Do unto others as you would have them do unto you," the Golden Rule of Communication is, "Only speak as you wish to be spoken to." Many a conflict could be avoided if we would all live by this rule.

Words can be very painful. Subsequently, marriage partners can be very cruel with their selection and presentation of words in the heat of the moment.

Think about it. Would you rather be...?

- **Preached** at or **Persuaded?**

- **Pushed** or invited to **Participate?**

- **Pounded** with facts or **Presented options?**

If you would rather not be preached at, pushed, or pounded with facts, chances are neither would your partner.

When my older two children were younger, I was prone to use some rather harsh words of correction. My daughter who was about 15 at the time remarked about how harsh I could be one time. I responded, "Yeah, but my bark is much worse than my bite." She then cut me to the quick, "Daddy, your bark is your bite."

That was an eye opener for this daddy. It was actually a turning point. Prior to that, I had prided myself in not using physical discipline often. I learned then that words can be more hurtful than swats.

Speak to your spouse in the same manner you would like to be spoken. Chances are they will return the favor.

Follow the THREE LAWS of COMMUNICATION:

If you do not take anything else away from this chapter except for these three laws, please take and apply them. Your communication will be revolutionized.

- **Say what you mean.** Think about it before you speak it. Don't say you will do anything that, realistically speaking, you know you can't or won't do.

- **Mean what you say.** If you say you are going to do it, make sure do it.

- **Never be mean with how you say it.** Basically, if you say what you mean and mean what you say, you really have no reason to *be mean* with how you say it.

I have been teaching these concepts to my clients for about a decade. I have received nothing but positive feedback.

Several years back, I received an opportunity to try them out for myself. I met my daughter and her friend for lunch. They left before I did. After a little while, my daughter's friend came back into the restaurant and told me I might better come out to the parking lot. Somebody had backed into my daughter and was trying to say it was her fault.

Understand, historically, if you wanted to get a rise out of me, all you had to do was mess with one of my kids. This time was different, though. I made a conscious effort to follow these three laws.

When I walked out the door, it was obvious this fellow had backed into my daughter. I walked up to him and my daughter and asked what was going on. The fellow responded, "It's really not a big deal. We just ran into each other. We both need to turn it in on our own insurance and collect on our own car."

I replied very calmly, "You are correct. It is not a big deal. You did not run into each other, though. You ran into my daughter. Consequently, we are turning it in on your insurance." At this, the fellow became very angry and argumentative.

I turned to my daughter as the fellow yelled threats and such at me. I told her to take the pictures we had already taken of the cars down to the fellow's insurer and see what they say. We then left with him standing there fuming.

The next day my daughter did as I said. She took her car and the pictures to his insurance agent. She left the office with a check in hand that covered the damage quite adequately.

I said what I meant, and I meant what I said, so I had no reason to be mean with how I said it. This works with strangers, our children, and our spouses. Give it a try.

Write LOVE LETTERS in Order to Clearly Communicate

Some things are just hard to say without risking being misunderstood. I personally on occasion like to put my words in writing. This gives me the opportunity to think my words through and choose the exact right words.

(Of course, the downside is, once you put it into writing you can't take it back. This is all the more reason to be careful with the words you choose.)

Here are some guidelines for writing a Love Letter:

- **Don't overdo it.** It is much more effective when done more conservatively, and maybe just on special occasions.

- **Focus on the good.** With practice, this can become a good way to point out the negatives without overstating them. When pointing out negatives, start out with words of praise, sneak in the negative toward the end, but always end with a positive. A good rule of thumb is to try to use 3 words of praise to every negative word.

- **Use 'makes me feel' statements.** Try not to accuse or criticize. Simply point out how their actions make you feel. An example might be, "When you raise your voice at me it makes me feel unloved." This would be as opposed to, "It is very unloving for you to yell at me." By the way, this technique is good to try verbally as well.

••

When I asked several happily married friends what the key to longevity of marriage was, one of the most common responses was communication. One of the leading causes of divorce is also communication or the lack thereof. It is not only important that what we say is right, but it is at least equally important that *how* we say it is right.

Pro 25:11

Activity that Promotes Longevity and Satisfaction...

Practice writing love letters to each other. Do not include negatives, though. Simply point out some positives. Be sure and use some "I" and feeling statements. Pick a quiet time alone to share the letters with each other. Follow it up with some non-verbal communication and end with an embrace.

Principle 8

CARING FOR ONE ANOTHER'S NEEDS

Just about the darkest days of my life were the days when I fell into the abyss of despair and anxiety a few years back. I truly lost all sight of hope and comfort during this time.

Nobody is sure what happened. It was probably a combination of the side effects of my medication and the onset of Parkinson's. Regardless of the cause, those days were very difficult for me, my family, and especially my wife.

I would awaken Kim at one or two o'clock in the morning desperate for her loving care. She would stay awake with me for the remainder of the night, comforting and reassuring me, totally disregarding her own need for sleep.

Kim gave us an excellent example of one caring for her spouse's needs at the expense of her own. When we exchange our marriage vows we normally promise to care for each other both "in sickness and in health and in poverty and in wealth." I interpret this to mean no matter the trials we face, the depths to which we fall, nor the anguish we experience, will we care for one another's needs.

I believe it was JFK that said, "Ask not what your country can do for you, but instead, what you can do for your country." This is the same attitude needed to determine the part you will play in your relationship.

Don't wait for a crisis to transpire in order to care or serve. Caring should be a daily routine. Caring is the act of love.

Gary Chapman in his book, "The Five Love Languages" (Moody, 2014), says there are five areas in which a person can show love or, in my terms, express care for another.

According to Chapman, each person has his or her own unique language:

- **Gifts**

    If your partner's love language is gifts, giving gifts is how you effectively show that you care. You might have flowers delivered to your spouse's workplace or bring home a box of candy. If you really mean business, you might even get them that watch they have been hinting about or surprise them by upgrading their phone.

- **Quality Time**

    This spouse desires your presence. You say "I love you" by going for a walk with them or by stopping by their workplace and taking them to lunch.

- **Words of Affirmation**

    This individual needs to hear your love and care for them. Tell them, "I love you," "I appreciate you," or "I am so sorry this happened to you." For this person, a love letter might be effective.

- **Acts of Service (Devotion)**

    To this person, you say you care by fixing a drink for them or taking out the trash. For a very special "I care" you might wax their car or mow the lawn for them.

- **Physical Touch (Intimacy)**

    Most guys are going to say, "Uh Yeah, this is me!" Not necessarily, though. This is about touching with no ulterior motives, just to say that you care.

I'm convinced most people need a combination of the above. We each have our preference, but all of us need a little of each from time to time. Ask yourself what there is that you can do to make your spouse's life better. What need have they expressed from time to time? What special deed can you perform that says, "I care about you"?

By the way, it's not always the big things that make the real difference either. Start small. Maybe buy them their favorite candy or fix them something to drink. Run an errand or simply pay them a compliment when maybe they expect it the least.

You know your partner's needs and wants better than anybody. Base your act of kindness on this time-acquired knowledge that only you might possess.

Understand, this act of kindness is most effective when it is totally unselfish. You give without expectations of receiving anything in return. You simply care because you care.

There are no doubt different ways to show one another you care. Nobody knows your partner better than you. Show them you care in a way that only you would know to do and only they would fully appreciate.

Eph 5:21-28

Activity that Promotes Longevity in Marriage...

Set a date a few days from now for a romantic outing. Each partner should decide on a secret act of kindness they can do for their partner between now and then. Each partner should try to figure out what the other's act of kindness is. Keep the act of kindness subdued, something they should appreciate, but do not overdo it. Plan a time during the date for the reveal.

Principle 9

HANDLE CONFLICT LIKE ADULTS

One of the scariest parts of an adoption home study is when the case worker interviews your existing children. In separate interviews during the process to adopt our youngest four children, the case worker once asked Dawn and Michael what their Mom and Dad argued most about. They both responded, "Silly things that don't really matter."

If you're around someone long enough, you are going to argue. Actually, you need to argue. Arguing is simply communicating when you disagree, and nobody agrees all the time.

The challenge is to argue correctly. By correctly, I mean productively and like mature adults. Argue to find the truth, not to win a battle of the egos.

Below are Four Steps to Handling Conflict Like Adults. I hope you will give these steps a try next time you disagree. If you do it right, you might even look forward to a disagreement on occasion.

1. Choose Your Corners

• Know Where You Stand

In order to argue, you must be willing to take a stand. Know what you believe and stand for what you believe.

• State it Clearly

Don't be ashamed of where you stand. If you don't proclaim it, they will never know it. State it clearly, but kindly. Make sure they understand where you are coming from.

• Stand Firm on the Truth

I talk of compromise and concession here soon. They are very important for consensus. Do not back down from the truth, though.

The truth is that part you know to be fact. Know where you draw the line, but be willing to give to that point and make sure that point is worth standing for.

2. Cover with Love

• Remain Calm

Don't get excited. This should be nothing personal. You are simply in search of the truth Yelling and raising your voice will do nothing but widen the gap between you and the one you love.

• No Criticism or Name Calling

As I said, this should be nothing personal. Focus on the issues, not the messenger. Be respectful even in your critique of their stand. Keep it pertinent and kind.

• Communicate Effectively

Follow the steps of communication outlined in Principle 7, particularly the three laws of communication. Remember, arguing is a form of communication. It is important that you communicate effectively to prevent misunderstanding and escalation.

3. Consensus, Not Conquest

• Consider Both Sides

There is no way to know your view is best until you consider first the other view. Seriously consider their view as the possible solution. Compare the two, noting the positives and negatives.

• Compromise Where Possible

The truth is usually found right in the middle between two opposing views. Don't be stubborn. Search for truth, not victory.

• Concede if Wrong

Don't be afraid to be wrong. Admit it. Embrace it. Confess it. It's not about being right. It's about discovering what's right. Usually compromise is the solution, but sometimes somebody just needs to eat some crow and admit they're wrong.

4. Conclude with an Embrace

The song says that, "The best part of breaking up is making up." Let's make that saying come true. After all, if you argue correctly, you deserve an embrace. Seriously, give yourself something to look forward to as you hash out your differences. Make all the hard work worthwhile. Why not give it a try?

Though conflict may not be desirable in marriage, it is inevitable. As long as we are putting two human beings together there will be conflict. I am not condoning it, but simply stating the obvious. Granted, the more consistently you apply the various principles I have covered, the less conflict you are liable to encounter. If you do encounter conflict, though, at least handle it like adults. No screaming, no name calling, and no slamming doors. Seek compromise, not conquest.

Eph 4:26

Activity that Promotes a Lasting Marriage...

There is no way I am going to challenge you to find something to argue about. You will do that soon enough on your own. Discuss the above guidelines and agree on your rules of engagement for your next disagreement. Sign the following contract. Practice your conclusion. Conclude with an embrace.

Couples Conflict Contract
Agreed Upon Between

_____ and _____

When two unique individuals enter into a relationship it is inevitable that conflict or disagreement will occur. It is not the absence of conflict but instead the handling of conflict correctly that strengthens a relationship. With that understood, we, the afore mentioned individuals, agree to abide by the following principles when disagreeing with one another. We will...

Choose our Corner
We will not concede what we strongly believe to be the truth. We will take a stand and communicate that stand clearly.

Cover with Love
We will not call names, criticize, and will remain calm. No yelling.

Consensus, not Conquest
Our goal is to discover the truth not to intimidate our partner.

Conclude with an Embrace
We will not let the sun set on our anger. Our goal will be to end every disagreement with an embrace.

Signed:

Husband:
_____

Wife:
_____

Principle 10

CONTINUE TO COURT

Do you remember that first flirtatious twinkle? How about that first touch, kiss, embrace? Do you remember the tingling you felt inside, all the way down to your toes?

What if I told you those special moments could be recreated? Well, they won't be the same. Honestly, though, if done right, they might be even better...different, but better.

Courting is a key to longevity and satisfaction in marriage. Don't let the flame go out. If it has dwindled already, rekindle it by courting each other much like you did in the beginning.

Schedule Special Time

Too often, once the vows are exchanged and the newness wears off, the couple starts losing focus and taking their relationship for granted. They begin focusing on the business of life - their education, their career, building a family, or their hobbies, etc.

All these are important and mostly necessary. We must be careful though not to neglect our relationship. Just as our career, children, and education require an investment of time, so does our marriage.

Finding time for one another can be difficult I know. It can be especially difficult once children enter the picture. It is absolutely necessary, though.

- **Daily Time**

Try to spend a little bit of quality time together on a daily basis. This may be a few minutes over breakfast before you awaken the kids or a moment of discussion as you drift off to sleep at night.

- **Date Night**

Plan a date night, weekly if you can or at least monthly. You might go to a movie or bowling, or you might just enjoy a quiet evening at home. Whatever you do, do it together.

- **Weekend Getaway**

Go camping or rent a hotel room in a nice resort town, or once again, spend a nice quiet weekend at home...alone. It is good if you can do this every 2-3 months, but at least a couple times a year.

Practice Chivalry

I once was told that chivalry was synonymous with chauvinism. That it was an insult for a man to hold the door for a woman or stand until she was seated. It insinuated she was not capable.

I differ. In the military, the lower ranking officer holds the door for the senior officer. He also stands when he enters the room. This is an act of honor.

Gentlemen, honor the one you love with chivalry. Open the door for her. Remove her coat for her. Hold her chair. Extend her the respect due her.

Ladies, allow your husband to be a gentleman. Hesitate and give him a chance to open the door or hold your chair, etc. Don't begrudge him for not, but at least give him the opportunity before moving on.

Chivalry isn't dead. Where it lives, so does romance.

Stir the Five Senses

There are at least five paths for saying, "I love you." These five paths are better known as the five senses. It is through the senses that we attract our mate.

This is true in the animal kingdom. The male peacock spreads his colorful feathers to attract a hen through the sense of sight. The bird has a distinct sounding chirp to call its mate. The buck is aroused by the smell of the doe in heat.

Do you recall the feeling you experienced the first time you observed your spouse walk into the room? What about the smell of his/her cologne or the taste of her lipstick?

The magic doesn't cease once you say "I do." Your spouse is still aroused or turned off by how you use the five senses to your advantage or disadvantage.

- **SIGHT** - You say I love you through sight by how you dress or take care of your body. You can experience the sense of sight by watching a sunset together or visiting an art museum.

    Kim and I celebrated our 30th anniversary in Hawaii. We enjoyed many wonderful activities while there. What we enjoyed most though was the scenery, especially the sunrise and sunset on the ocean.

- **HEARING** - Experience the sense of hearing by enjoying your favorite song together or at least your genre. Listen to the bird's chirp or the night sounds.

- **TOUCH - Hold** hands as you walk through the park. Run your fingers through each other's hair or snuggle on the couch. Offer a gentle touch as you meet each other in the hallway.

- **SMELL -** If you want to say I want you or I love you, first of all, make sure you don't stink. In other words, guys, take a shower. Secondly, wear his/her favorite cologne. Also, maybe burn his/her favorite smelling candle or incense.

- **TASTE -** Enjoy your favorite meal together or maybe your favorite drink. What did you have for dinner your fist date or honeymoon? Bring back special memories through your taste buds.

Confirm Your Love with Intimacy

I once had a struggling young couple come to me begging for help. They were on the brink of divorce. Her biggest complaint was all he ever wanted was sex. His complaint was she didn't seem attracted to him anymore. She never wanted sex.

They argued back and forth about what each of them perceived as the problem. After listening to them for a bit, I asked her to leave the room. I then challenged the husband to schedule a date night with his wife for the next week. Until then he was not to mention sex. Instead, he was to be extra courteous to her, helping with the dishes, picking up after himself, and maybe even serve her breakfast in bed.

On the date night, he was to lay the chivalry on thick. He was to open the door for her, get her coat for her, and buy her flowers. When they returned home, he still was not to bring up sex. If everything went as I hoped, he would not have to. She would, and it would most likely be some of the best most intense sex they had ever had. He was skeptical, but he agreed to give it a try.

I pretty much forgot about my challenge until I heard my phone ding with a text at 2 AM following their date night. It was from the husband. It read, "YOU WERE RIGHT!!!"

I do not do sex therapy. I do help people improve their relationships, though, which in turn improves their intimacy. It's not so much about what goes on in the bedroom, but instead what gets you there.

Three Keys to a Satisfying Sex Life:

1. Results from a Satisfying Marriage

A satisfying sex life is the result of doing marriage right, not the cause of it. If you want a better sex life, improve you relationship skills.

2. is Respectful

The best sex is aimed at satisfying your partner, mot yourself. You should never ask your partner to do something he/she is uncomfortable doing.

3. is Rewarding

Sex is a gift from God. He does not tell us how to do it. The only two rules are to be respectful and ENJOY!

****

It is important we court one another in the beginning. We lure one another in with kindness and chivalry. It is even more important to court the longer we are together. As time passes and our lives and what once attracted us to one another become mundane, not only is it important we court like we did in the beginning, it is important we court even more, different, and better.

Song of Solomon 7:6-12

Activity that Promotes Longevity in Marriage

Plan a weekend getaway. It doesn't have to be something special or expensive. It might be just sending the kids to Grandma's for the weekend and you staying home or leaving the kids at the house with a sitter while you find a motel room. You deserve a break, though, and you need the time alone.

Principle 11

HONOR YOUR COMMITMENT

My oldest son Michael was two years old and struggling with asthma. He had been to the doctor for testing, treatment, and such on seemingly a weekly basis. We had even feared for his life at times and had just recently ruled out a diagnosis of Cystic Fibrosis.

To make matters worse, I had just been discharged from the army and we had moved to Memphis to start a new life. I had yet to secure gainful employment. Of course, our finances were subsequently in crisis mode as well.

We had been living in an apartment in northern Memphis for about three months with nine months remaining on our lease. The apartment had a serious water leak that had led to mold, mildew, and Michael's hospitalization.

Our landlord refused to let us out of our lease until I finally made some serious phone calls. After some convincing, we were released.

Here's the kicker. We had to be out of our old apartment by midnight New Year's Eve. The home we were moving into wouldn't be ready until AFTER midnight. Did I mention it was cold and raining that night as well?

Well, this was a very stressful time for this young married couple. We weren't handling it well either. We snapped and yelled at each other all night long.

My parents were there helping us move that evening. My mom would later tell me that she and Dad really didn't expect our marriage to survive another year. At that moment, we weren't too sure we wanted it to survive another year.

That was 30 years ago and here we are, still together, more in love than ever before. We have weathered many more and even greater storms, ranging from unemployment and homelessness to death and chronic illness. Through it all, we have hung strong and come out that much stronger!

During the heat of the storm, you become tired of fighting. You feel as if you have gone as far as you can go. You just want to throw up your hands and give it up. It is at this point that many would file for divorce.

It is times like these though that you must dig your heels in that much further and say, "No way!" You must refuse to give in to the temptation to throw in the towel. You must stand strong on that commitment you made to each other and God, that commitment to hang in there 'for better for worse'...'to have and to hold from this day forward'.

In the midst of the struggles, there have been at least three pillars of strength we have hung onto to keep from being swept away by the storms of life. You too can find stability in these pillars:

- **Your HISTORY**

You have made it this far for a reason. There was something that pulled you together to begin with. You have had some awesome times together. Grab hold of that original attraction and recreate it. Remember the good times and the past accomplishments you have managed as well as the bad times you have weathered together. Remember the bad from the past and learn from it. Recall the good from your past and let it boost you into a positive future.

- **What You HAVE Now**

What do you have? Your family? Your children? Your job? Your hobbies? What about each other? We have a tendency to zero in on the bad and forget all the good in our lives. Focus on the good. Realize what you would be losing instead of gaining in a divorce. I am figuring it would be much. Embrace the good!

- **Your HOPE for a Better Future.**

Very often our marital struggles are not so much about each other. They instead are about our circumstances and life struggles. We simply tend to transfer our frustration with our life situation onto those we love.

Whatever it is you are struggling through now may very well fade in the future. Divorce is a permanent solution to what so often might have been a temporary problem.

Hold on for a better tomorrow. Look for that hope, that light, that glimpse of a better future. Let the light of tomorrow guide you through the struggles of today.

Love is most beautiful when it has weathered the storm.

You ever notice how dull the terrain is until the first storms of spring? It is only after the storms with all the winds and the rain that the true beauty of the outdoors is realized. Then suddenly, the trees are full, the grass is green, and the colorful flowers bloom.

Your love for a time will be dull and boring. At other times, it will be rocky and turbulent as it withstands the storms of life.

It is only after this time of boredom coupled with the tragedy of the storms of life that the true beauty of your love will shine through. Do not give up on your love before it has a chance to show its total beauty. May the beauty of your love shine through the storms of life.

The fact is a person is no better than his or her word. The opposite is true as well. Your word is no better than you. Sometimes, in the midst of struggles, disappointment, doubt, and even infidelity, all you have is your word and your commitment to stay together. Your word is a test of who you are. Pray to God that when all else has failed and gone, your commitment is enough.

Mar 10:9

Activity that Promotes Longevity and Satisfaction in Marriage

Discuss these following challenges. What can you anticipate that might test your commitment? Discuss the possible scenarios that might shake your foundation. What about the loss of a loved one? Loss of a job? Financial crisis? Addiction? Terminal or Chronic illness of either partner? What about boredom, apathy, or even infidelity? What would it take to cause even consideration of severing your commitment and going back on your word?

History - Discuss your beginnings, what you have overcome, and what has inspired you to hang on.

Here and Now – Discuss what is going on now that makes hanging on worth the effort.

Hope for the Future – Discuss what gives you as a couple hope for the future.

Principle 12

PERSEVERE THROUGH CRISIS

We once attended a church with a very wise pastor. The pastor was normally very positive and upbeat. We went into a building campaign though, in which he adopted Murphy's Law as the church's philosophy, *anything that can go wrong, probably will go wrong.*

This idea was not as negative as it might have seemed on the surface. The thought was if there is a chance something will go wrong, then why not prepare for it? If we are prepared for it, it may not be so wrong after all.

I assure you, in your marriage things will go wrong. I'm not being a pessimist. I'm just being a realist. It is best you prepare for the inevitable. If you are prepared for it, then when it actually happens it might not be so bad after all.

Learn Each Other's Crisis Mode

Everyone reacts to a crisis differently. Though some modes are more productive and healthier than others, there is no particularly right or wrong mode. Mostly, they just are what they are.

Whereas it might be helpful to work on adapting your own mode, more often than not it is going to be counterproductive to attempt to change your spouse's mode. There are several modes of reaction exhibited by various individuals in times of crisis. It is probably a good idea to understand your loved one's mode and know beforehand how you might interact with him or her in crises.

- **Anguish**

This person is liable to sleep a lot, cry, and even sink into clinical depression. As a spouse you need to be both understanding and supportive of this loved one during crisis.

- **Anger**

This individual is quick to snap. They are angry at the circumstances but are taking it out on those around them, especially those they love and trust the most. It is important that the recipient of this frustration not take it personal. It is actually an honor to be the one they trust enough to release their stress on. As hard as it might be, be patient and don't fight back. Reassure them and support them in this most difficult time. Hopefully, they will work their way through it. I assure you, if you snap back, it's only going to get worse.

- **Avoidance**

This person denies the problem even exists, either in word or action. They either doubt the event happened or they act as if they don't care. Don't be fooled by their facade though. They know and they care. They need you and they need you bad. Be there for them.

- **Anxiety**

This person is overwhelmed by the situation. They understand or even exaggerate the magnitude of it and cannot take their thoughts off it. They are overcome with fear and anxiety. They need you to be strong for them. Whatever you do, do not abandon them in their tremendous time of need.

- **Analytical**

This person remains calm and analyzes the problem looking for the solution. They may seem rather cold themselves, but in reality, they care dearly. Listen to them and trust them. Given the opportunity, they will lead you through the crisis unscathed. But also understand they are hurting too. Offer them the support they need.

LOOK for the Good

It is so easy to become obsessed with the negatives in life. In the midst of the storm we so often can perceive nothing but the thunder, lightning, and strong winds. We lose sight of the clothing we have to keep us dry, the shelter we have been able to find protection in, and the loved ones we find comfort in. We acknowledge only the storm.

You see, the solution cannot be found in the storm. The solution is in the good outside the storm. Look to the good for comfort in the midst of the storm. It is there you find the solution to the storm.

Love Each Other Through the Storm

When we are in the midst of crisis, our true loyalties often come out. It is during trauma that many often turn to drugs and alcohol. Others turn to work or recreation. Oftentimes, this is when unfaithfulness creeps in. The sad part is, instead of improving our situation, these crutches, addictions, or hideouts simply make it worse.

I officiated the wedding of a young couple a few years' back. Maddie and Dakota, like most newlyweds, were madly in love and had nothing but positive plans for their future. They had their first child within their first year of marriage. It was a beautiful healthy little girl they named Sophie. All was well…for the time.

Within just a few months, Maddie discovered she was with child again. This time, the pregnancy didn't go so well. Maddie's water broke at 16 weeks. Because of her lack of amniotic fluid, the baby's lungs were not developed properly and its frame and skull were weakened. The doctors said the child would likely not survive to term and if he did, he would no doubt be stillborn. They gave him no chance of survival.

One night well over two months before his due date, we received a call asking for prayer for Maddie, the child, and the family. Maddie had gone into labor. Kim rushed to the hospital to be with Maddie during this long dark night. I stayed home with our children.

I fully expected to be awakened to very grim news the following morning. Once again, the doctors gave no chance of survival. Instead of the grim news I expected though, Kim came beaming into the room at the break of dawn and announced that the baby was born and doing very well considering.

It was touch and go for several weeks, but all in all the baby progressed well. Of course, his health and frame were compromised and weakened, but he was progressing.

This was a very trying time for this young couple, more than most newlyweds could handle. Just as the baby's wellbeing had been touch and go, so had their relationship. They were surviving, though, until…

One morning when they went in to awaken Ben to get him ready for the day, they noticed things weren't quite right. He was listless and pale. They took him to ER to get him checked out, not knowing what was wrong,

During the exam, the doctor discovered a fracture in the baby's skull and immediately referred him to another bigger hospital in Tulsa. Upon their arrival at the hospital in Tulsa, the staff immediately called in child welfare. Not knowing the child's history (which would have explained the fragile development of the skull), the agency removed the child.

Though nothing was ever discovered to indicate foul play, the baby was removed from the mom and dad for over nine months. During this time, the young couple was not only separated from their child, but they were under constant intrusion, scrutiny, and investigation.

Dakota and Maddie's marriage was tested greatly during this time. The healthiest of couples would have faltered under such duress. I would like to say they stood strong throughout, but to be honest, there were numerous times I truly didn't think they were going to survive as a couple.

The fact is they did survive, though. No doubt they considered throwing in the towel, but they didn't. They held on tight to all that they had...God, each other, and their children.

Since the first writing of this book 3 years ago, the couple I told about above has divorced. They made it through the storm only to succumb to its pressures in the calm after the storm. I considered removing their story, but decided to leave it in as a reminder as to how difficult it can be to weather the storm.

When we go through trials, we are often tempted to part with what matters most, latching onto what matters least. Again and again, we see couples devastated by the storms or crisis in their lives.

One or both become distracted by the storm. They lose sight of their spouse. They lose sight of their love. In the end, they end up without the very one who understands their plight the most. The very love that is capable of bringing them through the storm they abandon to the storm.

On the reverse side of this, those who grasp hold of their love, those who embrace the one who understands them best, those who love their way through the storm, find a different kind of love, a higher level of love than they ever knew before. Before the storm, before the rain, the love is just a seedling, a sprout at best. It is through the storm that true love is formed. After the rain, after the calm, after the sun, it is then that that little sprout blossoms into a tremendous wholesome love that before could not have been imagined.

****

There is no doubt that as a couple you will face struggles. The question is not whether you will encounter crisis. The question is how will you react to it, what will you learn from it, and as a couple, how will you grow through it?

Rom 4:3-8

Activity that Promotes Longevity in Marriage

Discuss and determine each other's crisis mode and how each other's differing crisis mode might interact with the other during crisis. Determine together a predetermined plan how you might prevent escalation or conflict over differing crisis modes.

Principle 13

COVER EVERYTHING WITH LOVE

Love Defined

Love is no doubt the most difficult word to define in the English language, at least it is from my perspective. The various definitions I discovered all emphasized it as a feeling. The fact is though if love is only an emotion, its significance and dependability are greatly diminished. Feelings are not dependable and rely heavily upon circumstances as well as a person's physical and mental status and wellbeing at the moment.

Though I must admit love is partly a feeling, at the same time I also acknowledge it is much more than just an emotion. Love is a thought, a choice, an action, an ambition. Love is a noun, a verb, and an adjective. I wouldn't call this a definition, but Love as I see it is the motivating factor linking two individuals in a relationship that first attracts them to each other physically and/or emotionally, and then often progresses to greater depths of attraction to the point that each individual achieves completion of self only in relation to the other.

Love is perfected when each partner is more concerned with completing the other than having the other complete themselves.

I admit the above assessment is a bit much to follow or digest. In essence, what I am saying is, love is not simply a physical attraction, an emotional connection, or a social arrangement. Though all those interactions may be implicated by love, none of them standing alone defines love. Love instead is a commitment of one individual to another in a mutually beneficial relationship culminating ultimately in a willingness of one or either to sacrifice self for the benefit of the other.

Marriage without Love

We have discussed several principles key to satisfaction and longevity in marriage. It is no doubt important to choose the right partner and to put our family in perspective and our past behind us. We must practice effective communication and persevere through crisis as well. All these principles are useless though unless they are covered with love.

Not only is love the ultimate and most important principle, it is by love that the other principles receive their significance and purpose.

Love is the reason and motivation behind everything we do to better our relationship. Without love, our commitment and acts of caring are empty and without cause. Without love, our marriage is simply a contract of convenience. Without love your marriage might last, but without love, its endurance is simply misery endured.

Love Exemplified

When Kim and I met in that parking lot over thirty years ago we had no idea what life had in store for us. Two weeks later at a back-to-school retreat, the seeds of romance were planted. Within a few weeks, we were madly in love. Well, we were totally infatuated and couldn't imagine life without one another. As the story goes, within a year we were married.

We have faced disappointment, frustration, and financial ruin. We have faced opposition, sickness, and even the death of loved ones. Currently, we face my battle with Parkinson's disease, well, and even other battles I wish not to publish.

We have tested our commitment and weathered the storms of life. We have fought through conflict and cared for one another's needs. We have learned to communicate without words and continue to court and enjoy each other's company better than ever before.

We have followed and lived the principles of this book throughout our marriage. These principles have proven effective for us, as they can also prove effective for you. With Love, you have everything even in the midst of nothing. Without love, you possess nothing even in the midst of everything.

••

All the principles of this book are important, but the principle of love is the most important. Without love the other 12 principles are vain. The absence of the other 12 principles though is evidence that love does not exist. Love never fails.

Activity that Promotes Longevity in Marriage

Discuss the level of your love and commitment based on your adherence to the various principles outlined in this book. Where are your weaknesses? What are your strengths? What challenges have you overcome? What challenges might lie before you? What has brought you through the challenges? What will be your strength in the future?

www.ingramcontent.com/pod-product-compliance
Lightning Source LLC
Chambersburg PA
CBHW071519040426
42444CB00008B/1710